Invisible Paw Prints

ROB KORTUS

Best Wishes!

RKortus

ISBN: 0692763643
ISBN-13: 978-0692763643
Library of Congress Control Number: 2016914508

A gift for:

_____

From:

_____

Date:

_____

DEDICATION

To God: Thank You for all my blessings. I feel lucky and blessed to have had the privilege of working with dogs and meeting so many wonderful people who have become cherished friends.

To all dog-loving people who believe canine companions are part of the family and not possessions.

To all veterinarians, animal rescue shelter organizations, therapy-dog organizations, therapy-dog teams from around the globe, and the American Kennel Club (AKC): This book is dedicated to you all! Thank you for caring for God's precious canine companions!

Then God said, "Let the earth bring forth the living creature according to its kind: cattle and creeping thing and beast of the earth, each according to its kind"; And it was so.
Gen. 1:24

CONTENTS

Foreword   ix

Acknowledgments   xii

1   Sixteen Years Old and Growing Up Fast   1

2   Life Is Too Short Not to Give Back a Little   6

3   A New Journey   13

4   Sophie…an Inspiration   20

5   A Moment   25

6   Paws Up   52

7   Life Is Golden   58

8   Read a Book…to a Dog   44

9   Smiling Eyes   49

10   Our Precious Children   54

11   The Amazing Grace   61

12   A Tear   72

13   Heartstrings   76

14   Children Are like Puppies   80

15   Paula's Best Friend   84

16 Unconditional Love   91

17 A Touch   95

18 Loss and Gain   103

19 I Want to Become a   111
    Registered Therapy-Dog
    Team

20 Invisible Paw Prints   115

    About the Author   120

Invisible paw prints.

FOREWORD

Many of the clients and students who have graduated from my dog-obedience classes ask what they can do with their dogs now that their dogs are so well behaved. Many of them ask about volunteering with their dogs. I always suggest pet therapy. However, I really can't explain what they will encounter when they take their dogs to a nursing home, hospital, or children's home.

Rob Kortus has answered their questions with his amazing book, *Invisible Paw Prints*. After reading the book, I was left with a beautiful feeling of how people can satisfy their desire to help those suffering with pain, loneliness, or disability, while including the dogs they love.

After spending over twenty-seven years in military aviation, Rob retired, adopted Sophie, a border collie, and started teaching her amazing tricks. Along with becoming a master dog educator/trainer, Rob started his own dog training business, Commander in Leash Dog Obedience and Behavior Training, and, with Sophie, started their dog-therapy team. Today, Rob teaches people and their dogs how to become a team.

People today are looking for activities that will involve their dogs. The bond between human and dog has become very strong. Strong in a different way than it used to be. Dogs were bred to work, hunt, herd, track, and guard. Now dogs are left home alone while their owners are working. The guilt many people feel can be overwhelming, especially when they come home to torn-up couches or dogs that have been in crates all day.

Many of the clients and students who have graduated from my Canine Good Citizen dog-obedience classes ask what they can do with their dogs. I tell them that their dogs would make good therapy dogs. But what is a therapy dog? What is required? How would the dog's owner be involved? Rob Kortus explains what it takes to be a therapy dog and how the dog's owner is involved. He calls dog and owner a team, a therapy team.

Invisible Paw Prints takes us through the Levine Children's Hospital, a nursing home, an assisted living home, Holy Angels, a camp for children with heart problems, even a library where children build their reading skills by reading to therapy dogs. We see how the eyes of suffering adults and children can quickly change to smiles when Sophie lays her head on their laps.

Read this book with gratitude, for this book is showing the way to a better life for you, your dog, and people who really need love. I'm honored to have been asked to write a foreword for as fine a book as *Invisible Paw Prints*.

Joan Lask
Owner & Director
Jo Thor's Dog Trainers' Academy

ACKNOWLEDGMENTS

Thank you to my mom and dad (Emiko and Richard) for showing me how to be a good, honest man. Thank you for teaching me discipline, respect, and integrity, and for introducing me to our first canine companion, Frenchie. Thank you for teaching me to care about those who are less fortunate. Thank you to my aunt Mutsuko for helping raise me and my two brothers.

Thank you to my brothers, Bobby and Rene, for your love and friendship, especially in our younger years and before Bobby passed on and went to heaven. Thank you to my sons, Stuart and Sean, for loving me unconditionally and for supporting me in all my endeavors.

Thanks to Charlie's Angels Animal Rescue for allowing me to work alongside them to train the helpless rescues to be better canine companions and more prepared for adoption. Thank you to Brother Wolf Animal Rescue for allowing me to adopt Sophie the border collie, my inspiration to become a dog trainer. Thank you to the Atlanta Humane Society (Mansell Campus) as well for the adoption of Sulley the chocolate Lab mix. A special thanks to Elizabeth for placing Wallace the chocolate border collie in my possession.

A very special thanks to Joan Lask, Sean Killoran, and Lorenzo Billups at the Jo Thor's Dog Trainers' Academy in Alpharetta, Georgia, for your guidance and expertise.

To Teresa McCarter and her son Brian McCarter, owners of the best dog boutique and spa in the Southeast, the Happy Dog Café Boutique & Spa Inc. in Belmont, North Carolina, for allowing me the wonderful opportunity to expand my dog-training business with group training at your gorgeous facility. I am forever grateful.

A very special thanks to all of my clients who trusted in my dog-training company to change both their personal lives and their canine companions' lives.

To Sharon Towers Retirement Community and CaroMont Regional Medical Hospital for allowing therapy-dog testing in your facilities.

Thank you to the following people and organizations and their staff, including those who were kind enough to allow therapy-dog visits:

Say "thank you" to someone every day of your life. Rob

- Dr. Edward M. Lineberger and staff at Lineberger Veterinarian Hospital, Gastonia, North Carolina

- Dr. Richard Hovis and staff at Dickson Animal Hospital, Gastonia, North Carolina

- Christopher Perez, Sam Coniglio, and Tucker Summerville at Levine Children's Hospital, Charlotte, North Carolina

- Joanne Sigmon, Susie Schronce King, Chrissy Byars, Tia Adams, Brittany Peeler, and Rachel Eldridge at Holy Angels, Belmont, North Carolina

- Julie Young and Traci Agnew at CaroMont Health, Gastonia, North Carolina

- Elizabeth Byrd, Aubrie Murphy, Stacy Flemming, and Whitney Fleming at Sharon Towers Retirement Community, Charlotte, North Carolina

- Jessie Craig at Florence Crittenton Services, Charlotte, North Carolina

- Kim Burke at Courtland Terrace Nursing Home, Gastonia, North Carolina

Credits: Bible quotes taken from the New International Version (NIV) and the New King James Version (NKJV).

1. SIXTEEN YEARS OLD AND GROWING UP FAST

The doctor picked up the razor-sharp scalpel from the stainless-steel table and began an incision into the queen; he then handed me one of the newborn kittens he had just taken from the queen's womb while conducting a C-section. He told me to place the kitten in both palms with the kitten lying on her back facing me and then make an upward and downward swinging motion with both arms high in the air and then down between my legs. This motion would help in removing mucus from the lungs of the newborn kitten. *Gently* holding the kitten, I began this swinging motion.

On the third upswing, the kitten flew out of my hands and hit the wall, bouncing off the ceiling and landing on the operating-room floor. I stood in disbelief. My heart sank. I did not know what to do, and I felt frozen in time.

I picked up the kitten and held it in my hands. Its breathing was slow and erratic. Then the breathing stopped. I had just inadvertently killed this newborn kitten. I teared up, feeling absolutely terrible. I was sixteen years old and working a part-time job at my local veterinary hospital. I would work here for two years.

A client brought the family dog to the hospital, and the doctor asked me to take the customer's canine companion back into the surgical room. I placed the dog on the stainless-steel table and waited for the doctor to arrive. As I waited, I played with and petted the happy and playful dog. When the doctor arrived, he began to explain that the dog was to be euthanized. My immediate thought was that the dog had some kind of terminal illness. So, I asked why we were euthanizing the dog.

"There is nothing wrong with the dog," the vet said. "The owners can no longer have the dog, and they do not want to give the dog away knowing it could be potentially abused." The wheels were turning in my head, attempting to understand the logic of this decision.

The doctor asked me to prepare the cephalic vein on the right arm of the dog. I had the dog's left ribs against my lower abdomen and with my right hand rolled my thumb over the cephalic vein in a rotating motion, revealing the injection point. He inserted the needle and then, as if in slow motion, began pressing the syringe plunger, injecting the overdose of cocktail into the dog's vein. Within seconds the dog slowly fell limp in my arms, and with tears in my eyes, I laid him on the cold stainless-steel table. My head moved upward to the doctor's gaze. The doctor then took his stethoscope to check for any heartbeat. I stood there still baffled and not understanding what had just taken place.

A man brought in a cardboard box containing a small dog. He said that he had found his dog in its current state. At first glance the dog appeared dazed, lying quietly in the box. Closer examination revealed that the dog was covered in fleas. Covered in hundreds of fleas! I recalled taking a stick and stirring up an ant pile when I was a young boy. Hundreds of ants scurried to the surface; it looked like the ground was moving. This was the visual I was seeing in front of me.

The doctor sprayed the body of the dog with flea spray. Like a water sprinkler, the fleas began to stream off the dog and into the air. It was a terrible sight. The doctor then rolled the jowls of the dog upward. The dog's gums were nearly white. Countless fleas were sucking the life out of this poor young dog. I then carried the pup into the surgical room.

The doctor filled the syringe with the cocktail overdose, placed the needle near the chest of the dog, and inserted the needle directly into the heart. The dog didn't even twitch. He simply slumped over in his little resting place, the cardboard box. I was saddened that day and angered that the dog had been left in this condition by his owner.

I have carried these events with me to this day. I remember them all as if they just happened yesterday. Working at a veterinary hospital as a young man was one of the best learning experiences I have ever had. Perhaps it was my transition from teen to man. There were many more happy and sad experiences like those mentioned above, but this is where my love for animals began.

"I remember all of these events as if they just happened yesterday."

Let no one despise your youth, but be an example to the believers in the word, in conduct, in love, in spirit, in faith, in purity.

1 Tim. 4:12

2. LIFE IS TOO SHORT NOT TO GIVE BACK A LITTLE

I landed the coast guard helicopter for the final time. I stepped out of the helicopter, knowing my journey assisting those individuals at sea during Homeland Security missions, drug interdiction, and a final staff job were behind me. A new journey was in my future. At the time, I did not know what this journey might entail. Only God and his Son knew.

After twenty-seven-plus years flying helicopters, I took the first year off after hanging up my flight suit and rode my Trek carbon fiber bicycle in the mountainous terrain of Asheville, North Carolina, where I had settled at that time, nearly every day for a year. My plan was to work for no one except myself. How that would happen, I did not know, and I did not care during that first year of relaxation.

The day after retirement, I told God I would give back even more since he protected my crews and me on every mission we flew. I decided to give back more financially when I could and to give more time as a volunteer.

My volunteer efforts began years ago as my parents and church always taught me to give back. I formulated the motto "Life is too short not to give back a little" after a trip to Belize, where I volunteered and brought donations from the United States for the Holy Family RC Primary School and volunteered time with the Hopkins Belize Humane Society's veterinary clinic with manager Kelli and vet tech Joseph, including dog training with some locals. The week-long trip was only for volunteering and giving back.

You see, there is something about volunteering that calms me and soothes my heart as if it is the natural thing to do. Like food and water, these basic necessities make me feel alive. Giving back has become a basic necessity in my life. It's solely about giving back after being so blessed all my life. It simply feels right.

I have volunteered over the years with many organizations for time periods of one day to several years and want to share just a few of them. Perhaps you, the reader, can find interest in some of these organizations or venture out on your own to find an organization that suits your interests.

Isaac and his puppy learning basic dog obedience in Belize.

The Relatives, a homeless teen shelter, Charlotte, North Carolina. Invited my loyal friends to cook meals on Thanksgiving Day and deliver to shelter.

Samaritan's Purse Operation Christmas Child shoe box gift program, Charlotte. Volunteered with friends packing shoe boxes for overseas destinations.

Big Brothers/Big Sisters (BBBS), Asheville. Board of directors/advisory council member. Volunteered as a big brother for a ten-year-old youngster (Dominique Jamerson), with whom I still remain in contact to this day. A quick shout out to Jill Hartmann for matching me up with little brother Dominique.

Veterans Restoration Quarters, Asheville Buncombe Community Christian Ministries (ABCCM), a homeless shelter for veterans, Asheville. Volunteered and served as an advisory council member.

Make a Wish, Charlotte office. Allocated a percentage of sales from my company JerseyBin.com as a Christmas donation that enabled a youngster to visit Walt Disney World.

Animal Compassion Network, Asheville. Volunteered as a home inspector, conducting home safety inspections for newly adopted dogs and cats to ensure the new environment was clean and safe.

Buncombe County Council on Aging, Asheville. Assisted seniors with yard work and minor home repairs and brought along my little brother Dominique (BBBS) on several occasions to learn about volunteering.

Coast Guard (CG). Volunteered as a pallbearer for two World War II CG commanders laid to rest at Arlington National Cemetery.

Special Olympics. Volunteered for two special Olympic games while in the CG. Heartwarming experience, to say the least.

Partnership in Education, H. L. Trigg Elementary, Elizabeth City, North Carolina (an after-school program). Assisted with reading and teaching sports. Awarded the Business Partner of the Year award.

YMCA Strong Kids Fund Raiser Wellness Committee, Asheville. Served on committee.

Local community intramural baseball and football youth league, Virginia. Served as assistant coach.

Washington, DC, soup kitchen. Volunteered with my office staff; prepared food for the homeless.

Charlie's Angels Animal Rescue, Fletcher, North Carolina. Set up a dog-in-training program. Trained rescued dogs with basic obedience, making them more desirable for adoption.

Then I found another way of giving back.

"Life is too short not to give back a little."

In everything I did, I showed you that by this kind of hard work, we must help the weak, remembering the words Lord Jesus himself said: "It is more blessed to give than to receive."

Acts 20:35

3. A NEW JOURNEY

Border collies are rated as the smartest breed of dogs in the world. They have high energy and are constantly thinking. No other breed of dog has the intellectual capacity of a purebred border collie. They are expert problem solvers who can solve complex tasks. This brings me to a well-known border collie named Chaser I saw on the Internet. She learned over one thousand words. Yes, I said over one thousand words. I had wanted a border collie of my own for many years.

I was relaxing while sitting on my couch watching television. A *feeling* came across me to go to Brother Wolf Animal Rescue in Asheville, North Carolina. I knew of this organization but had never visited. A half hour went by, and then an hour, and the feeling (this sorta nudge) grew stronger and stronger. Consequently, I put on my tennis shoes, tied the laces, grabbed my truck keys, and headed out to the rescue shelter, uncertain of what was going on with this nudge.

As I stepped out of my truck, I heard barking from inside the facility. You could ascertain by the sound of the barks that the dogs were stressed. I reached for the worn doorknob, turned it, and slowly opened the door. As I approached the counter, the employee asked if she could help me. I replied that I just wanted to browse the facility to see the dogs that were available for adoption. I accessed the main room through another door. I opened the door, so the dogs could see me, and the barking increased tenfold.

As I stood in place taking in all the sights and smells, I was thinking there would not be a border collie in this rescue facility, especially not a purebred. I began a slow walk and passed several kennels with small dogs. The look of desperation was in their eyes. My heart was feeling the pain of their predicament, stuck in a small cage watching humans walk by daily. It made me wonder what a dog might say to a passerby.

As I stopped and turned to my left, in the distance I saw a black-and-white dog housed in a chain-link enclosure. I began to walk in the direction of this dog. Once I arrived at the enclosure, I noticed this dog appeared to be very shy. My eyes went from this dog to a small piece of paper about head high on the gate of the enclosure. Name: Sophie. Breed: border collie. Age: ten to twelve months. I peered back down at this skinny border collie. She looked up at me with these sad eyes as if to send me a quiet hello. She seemed nervous and obviously undernourished.

I walked back out to the front counter and inquired about Sophie. The employee stated that Sophie had been brought in just a few days ago and appeared to be about ten months old. No one had claimed her, and she did not have a microchip.

One of the first photos of Sophie at the age of one year.

Found alone in the woods in Tennessee, Sophie was brought down to Asheville. I asked if I could take her for a walk. I returned through the gauntlet of rescued dogs, odors, and noisy barking and approached Sophie's kennel. She cowered when the leash was attached to her collar. We walked out of the facility, away from her noisy temporary home and friends.

Sophie seemed to perk up a little bit outside, away from the noisy confines of the rescue shelter. We walked around, and I sat down alongside her several times during our first walk together. She would lean her head and body against me. I noticed something very interesting with Sophie. When she would stand on her hind legs and place her paws on me, she would curl her paws downward as not to place her paw pads and nails against my thighs.

After spending about fifteen minutes together, I walked Sophie back to her kennel. As I released her and closed the gate, our eyes met again, and she looked at me as if to say, "Are you going to take me home?" I did not take her home with me.

The following day I returned to the rescue facility and asked if I could walk Sophie again. Entering the noisy and dog-odor-filled kennel area, I looked at Sophie. As I got closer, her gaze set on mine, and I saw some tail wagging. When I began to clip her collar to the leash, she gave me a couple of licks on the forearm. We then proceeded outdoors. We walked a bit longer this time, and I talked to her as if I were talking to a friend. Where exactly did you come from? Who was your owner? How did you survive? What is your story?

We trekked back inside the rescue facility, and again Sophie gazed at me with those sad eyes as if to say, "Are you leaving me again?" I headed home that morning to think about adopting Sophie. Later that day I called and advised the staff that I would like to adopt her. They were as delighted as I was. I told them I would pick her up the following morning.

Remember that *nudge* I spoke of, when I was sitting on the couch watching television, to go to Brother Wolf Animal Rescue? It was God nudging me. No doubt in my mind. He directed me to this canine companion for a reason. To rescue this poor soul from death and *to start a new journey.*

"A half hour went by, and then an hour, and the feeling (nudge) felt stronger and stronger."

I give Sophie a kiss after a wonderful therapy-dog visit at Sharon Towers Retirement Community.

Rescue those who are being taken away to death, hold back those who are stumbling to the slaughter. If you say, "Behold, we did not know this," does not he who weighs the heart perceive it? Does not he who keeps watch over your soul know it, and will he not repay man according to his work?

Prov. 24:11–12

4. SOPHIE…AN INSPIRATION

Sophie was my inspiration to become a certified professional dog trainer. I attended Jo Thor's Dog Trainers' Academy in Alpharetta, Georgia. The academy is owned and operated by nationally known dog trainer Joan Lask. After over twenty-four hundred hours of training, I received four certifications, including the advanced dog educator/trainer certification.

With decades of experience in dog training and behavioral modification, founder Joan Lask also trained dogs for several movies, including *The Nightman*, *The Two Tonys*, and *Fried Green Tomatoes* (farm animals). Some commercials on which she worked include the Bell South Yellow Pages Ad with Dixie Carter from *Designing Women*, Ford Motor Company, NAPA Auto Parts, Cumberland Mall (Atlanta, Georgia), Town Center Mall (Kennesaw, Georgia), McKenzie Frozen Foods, Network Rental, Stanley Tools, Aaron Rents, First American Bank, Bank South, Petstuff, and the Georgia Lottery.

Joan has trained animals for live theater and the Atlanta Opera. She has done print ads for Weiman Homes, Storehouse Furniture, and others. She has trained dogs for circus acts, participated in fashion shows, and has been interviewed on radio. In addition, Joan has been featured on news specials on Atlanta's Channel 5 and Channel 2 News at noon, the *Healthy Home Show*, and a TBS special.

When I first began attending the academy, I started my dog-training business, Commander-in-Leash Dog Obedience & Behavior Training, at about the same time. I think Joan and instructor Sean thought I was a bit nuts to do so. I set up the website and applied for and received the trademark Commander in Leash. As I trained with my first clients, I trained at no charge so I could practice my new craft. After several months of working with local clients, I would charge ten dollars a lesson. By the end of the course, I began charging competitive pricing in my area.

Author at Jo Thor's Dog Trainers' Academy

My business has been successful for several reasons. I emphasize world-class training through the Jo Thor Dog Trainers' Academy and hard work and dedication to my clients. In addition, the business is well known through word of mouth by my clients and especially because of Teresa and Brian McCarter at Happy Dog Café, Boutique & Spa, Inc., Dr.

Edward Lineberger and his staff of Lineberger Veterinarian Hospital, and Dr. Hovis of Dickson Animal Clinic. They all kindly send their clients my way should the clients require dog training or dog behavior modification. I am so grateful and so blessed.

What I didn't realize at the time—that year off after retiring from flying and riding my bike up and down steep climbs of the Blue Ridge Mountains in Asheville—was that later, I would become a certified professional dog trainer. It was a new journey, a new beginning because of the inspiration that came from my loyal canine companion, Sophie.

"I think Joan and instructor Sean thought I was a bit nuts to do so."

I can do all this through him who gives me strength.

Phil. 4:13

5. A MOMENT

Sophie, the rescued border collie became a registered therapy dog. You see, a therapy dog such as Sophie leaves behind no paw prints, only trails of human smiles, happiness, hope, and love. She will leave invisible paw prints in every facility she visits.

I noticed a hospital volunteer sitting near the entrance of a patient's room. I peeked inside and saw a man lying on his bed, reading a Bible that was open on his wheeled tray. He was covered up to his chest with white hospital sheets, and his head was cocked downward. I was unable to see his eyes, but he appeared to be in deep thought with his Bible.

I advised the hospital volunteer director, Julie Young, who was with me, that the patient was reading his Bible, and we should probably not disturb him. As we started to walk away from his room, something (a nudge) told me to go into this particular room with Sophie. So I advised the volunteer director that something was telling me to visit this man, turned around, and approached his hospital room doorway.

I saw the man's right leg partially uncovered by the white sheets, and I saw an ankle bracelet monitor. As my gaze moved upward, I saw several IV connectors on the man's right arm. My eyes passed over the man's unshaven face, as he was still reading his Bible, and I saw an oversized bandage around the man's left wrist. I gently spoke and asked the man if he would like a therapy-dog visit. His head raised up ever so slowly when he heard me, and he said, "Sure." His hands moved from each side of the Bible, coming to rest side by side on top.

I entered the small hospital room, walked around the left side of the man's bed, and introduced myself and Sophie. As if on cue, Sophie quickly stood on her hind legs with her front paws on the bedside so the man could reach her head and pet her. He cracked a bit of a smile as Sophie licked his arm.

I asked him if he was enjoying his Bible. He said yes, and we began to talk. I told him my story and about God's nudges to get me off the couch several years ago to visit an animal rescue shelter, where I found and adopted Sophie. Then I spoke of how Sophie had touched so many lives as a therapy dog.

In a weary and tentative soft tone, he told me he recently attempted to kill himself. My eyes were directed to his brown eyes as he said, "I just wanted to die." He had lost his home and all his belongings in a fire and had been living on the streets. With no identification cards, he was struggling to find a job. He was a welder. As he was telling me his story, I could see and feel the pain he was going through. As he stroked Sophie's head, he said he had been through many tough times and at this point, he simply wanted to die.

He found God through some other homeless people he had met. He said in the past he would give small amounts of money to the homeless or just a slice of pizza to the hungry. I began to sense that this man had a wonderful heart. He was one of God's children who didn't have much but would still give.

He went on to say that he was in his bathroom on that dreadful day when he was cutting his wrist to end his life. Blood was everywhere. His friend heard some commotion in the bathroom and voiced concern to his friend. The man told him not to enter, but his friend kicked the door in, and the man began to fight his friend. The man then woke up staring at the roof of an automobile with strangers around him and a siren in the background. He was being saved by the ambulance crew.

I told the man that God sent his friend to his house in order to save his life. I told him of a good Christian friend, Karen, who lost her twelve-year-old son. Kevin was struck and killed by a drunk driver while walking across a road with his older brother four days before Christmas. It was late at night, and the drunk driver did not have his headlights on. Kevin and his brother never saw the vehicle coming. The doctors wanted Karen to take several drugs that would calm her nerves. She rejected the doctor's recommendation and found her strength through God.

I wanted to let him know that many people have had extremely difficult times in their lives. Karen turned to God to get her through her devastating loss. I told him to seek God's glory and strength, and God would help him get through this period of his life. I suggested he continue to frequent his church to gain support from his fellow Christians through fellowship. I went on to say that God saved him and wanted him to be here on this earth for a reason and only he could find out what that was.

What felt like an hour was probably only about twenty-five minutes with this man. I said my good-bye as he gave Sophie one last touch, and Sophie and I moved from the side of the bed and out of the hospital room.

There I found the volunteer director, in tears, leaning against the hall wall. I asked Julie what was wrong. She said she had listened intently to the entire conversation while standing outside the hospital room, out of view. The dialogue had deeply touched her heart.

She told me how about halfway through the conversation, the man's voice inflection and tone changed from soft and withdrawn to confident as we spoke more and more. She said that I have a certain "light" in my heart. I was grateful for the comment and told her that this was what therapy-dog teams are all about. *It wasn't at all about me, it was all about Sophie.* People who have fallen ill sometimes simply need a "moment."

Pastor Steven Furtick of Elevation Church once said, "It is the moments that seem insignificant that prepare us for the moments that are most significant…when what you're doing seems insignificant, but the cause you're doing it for is significant, then what you are doing takes on supernatural significance for the glory of God." This perspective makes great sense.

I shared my good-bye with the volunteer director and headed down the long hall to the hospital exit. As I strolled slowly down the hall, I reflected on the experience I had just had and began to tear up as I thought about this man. My view of the revolving doors was blurred by my tears. I was touched by his story and felt assured that God had *nudged* me to go back and enter this man's hospital room.

This man, this complete stranger, simply needed a *moment*. Sophie gave this to him through her presence, licks, and being petted. The volunteer director indirectly had her *moment*. Sophie gave this to her. We all can make a difference. Sometimes people just need a *moment*.

"He found God through some other homeless people he had met."

The righteous cry out, and the Lord hears them; he delivers them from all their troubles. The Lord is close to the brokenhearted and saves those who are crushed in spirit. The righteous person may have many troubles, but the Lord delivers him from them all; He protects all his bones, not one of them will be broken.

Ps. 34:17–20

6. PAWS UP

After working with Sophie as a therapy-dog team, I wanted to somehow promote and share this volunteer lifestyle with other canine lovers. So I submitted my paperwork to become a therapy-dog tester and observer with a therapy-dog organization.

After taking an online test, I became a therapy-dog tester and observer. This was an all-volunteer program. After a therapy-dog team passes its handler's test and three observations, the team sends in the required documentation along with the annual membership fee. The new therapy-dog team receives a certificate and a heart-shaped dog tag, and the handler receives an ID card. More important, the therapy-dog company provides liability insurance for the new team.

When I train canines through my dog-training business and find those I believe would make great therapy dogs, I always recommend this wonderful volunteer opportunity to the client and explain how painless the process is to become a therapy-dog team. In addition, I explain the amazing journey they will experience as they venture out on their own and meet so many remarkable and interesting people and hear their stories.

I remember one of the first therapy-dog teams I tested, Tekla and Cammie. Tekla had a beautiful yellow Lab. The team tested with perfection and easily conducted the facility observations with little coaching. I was so proud of the team when they completed the registration process. To this day, they continue to volunteer as a therapy-dog team, and Tekla has many stories to share about their journey.

As I explain to all new therapy-dog teams, they will be on a journey of various emotions, depending on the type of facility they volunteer for. As you will read later, visiting Levine Children's Hospital can be emotional not only because the teams visit children suffering from various medical issues, but also they see their families having to watch their children suffer and in some instances pass away.

Tekla was volunteering with Cammie at a local hospital, and as she was walking the halls, a young woman approached her. She said her sister, who was a patient, was dealing with declining health and increasing depression. The woman went on to say that her sister had not spoken to anyone in three to four days. She asked Tekla to visit with Cammie. Tekla accommodated this request.

Tekla and Cammie entered the small hospital room and slid the privacy curtain to the left to approach the bed. Tekla glanced to her left and saw the IV stand with multiple medical devices and wires hanging on it like ornaments on a Christmas tree. Then Tekla saw the patient lying on her back with her arms relaxing on each side of her body. She was covered with a sheet and blanket over the lower half of her body, along with two soft pillows on each side of her waist. In Tekla's peripheral vision, she could see some of the family members near the foot of the bed.

When Tekla's gaze met the patient's, the patient's eyes widened with a seemingly confused expression as if to say, who might you be? With a beautiful smile, Tekla spoke softly and introduced herself as a volunteer. Cammie was hidden by the height of the bed, waiting to do her work.

Tekla calmly commanded Cammie, "Paws up!" Cammie stood on her hind legs, popped her head up, and draped her paws over the bed railing. Not knowing Cammie was present until that moment, the patient smiled with glee, reached over, caressed Cammie's paw, and spoke the words, "Oh, such a sweet baby!"

The room fell silent for just a few seconds, and as Tekla glanced at the family members, she saw tears of joy. Tears of joy created by the *magic* of a therapy-dog team. Tekla had one of those wonderful, heartfelt, therapy-dog team moments.

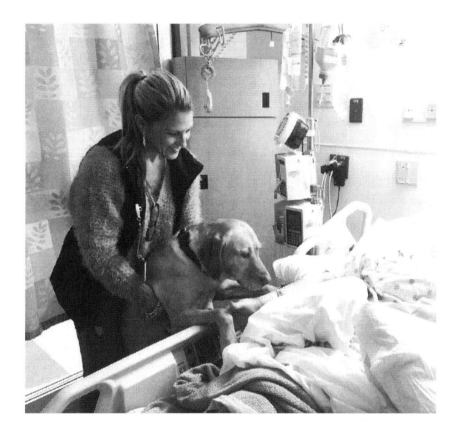

Therapy-dog team Tekla and Cammie are in volunteer mode, making magic.

Powerful moments like this may make many of you wonder how to get started as a therapy-dog team. At the end of this book, I will discuss what it takes to become a therapy-dog team. It is simple. It only takes some time and effort on your part, and the journey will be rewarding, I promise.

"Not knowing Cammie was present, the patient smiled with glee, reached over, caressed Cammie's paw, and spoke the words, 'Oh, such a sweet baby!'"

The stranger who dwells among you shall be to you as one born among you, and you shall love him as yourself; for you were strangers in the land of Egypt: I am the Lord your God.

Lev. 19:34

7. LIFE IS GOLDEN

I met Nikole and Charlotte, Nikole's golden retriever, at Sharon Towers Retirement Community for their final observation to become a registered therapy-dog team. After entering the retirement home, we began to roam the halls to make visits. Our first stop was the patio.

Nikole and Charlotte after their final observation before certification.

We peered through the glass doors and saw that two of the staff members were singing and playing the guitar for about a dozen of the residents. Nikole and Charlotte were waved at to come in and join the residents, all sitting comfortably in their wheelchairs and patio chairs.

I witnessed many happy faces as the residents caressed Charlotte. At the same time, Nikole would smile and speak to each of the residents. It is absolutely beautiful to watch when a therapy-dog team so effortlessly affects the lives of so many. I caught myself grinning from ear to ear, watching this beautiful team volunteering their time to bring joy to others.

After the patio visit, we wandered from room to room. We met Dave, who was visiting a resident. Dave read us all a poem he recently wrote called "A Summer's Day." It was beautiful. Dave mentioned to Nikole that he too used to have golden retrievers and missed them. Dave told Nikole he was inspired by her visit with her golden retriever and was inspired to write a poem about goldens.

Not more than twenty-five minutes later, as Nikole and I were sitting down in the lobby completing the therapy-dog testing paperwork, Dave appeared. He told Nikole he had written the poem.

We were astonished that this man had drafted a poem so quickly. With Nikole standing on his right side and Charlotte sitting directly in front of Dave staring up at him, he began to recite his poem.

"Goldens"

If humans could learn to love
as absolutely
as unconditionally
as joyfully
as a golden retriever
What a wonderful world it would be.

If humans could trust each other
as selflessly
as instantly
as completely
as a golden retriever
What a world of peace we would have.

And if humans had such love
And such trust
Their eyes would shine with joy whenever

they would see each other
and their tails would always wag
and life would be
just GOLDEN!

(Author: Dave Mitchell)

Nikole is a very special young woman. She has her own story that puts her on a very personal journey in life. She has a great understanding of how precious life is, and perhaps that is why she is giving back through starting a therapy-dog team. Learn more about Nikole's story through the use of the below QR code.

I tell every therapy-dog team that is testing that they will be on a very special journey. On that journey they will hear many stories, share some of their own stories, and even shed a tear. The impact of a therapy-dog team will not only affect those whom they visit but also the therapy-dog team themselves. It is sometimes a roller coaster of emotions. It is a blessing.

"It is absolutely beautiful to watch when a therapy-dog team so effortlessly affects the lives of so many."

For you created my inmost being; you knit me together in my mother's womb. I praise you because I am fearfully and wonderfully made; your works are wonderful; I know that full well.

Ps. 139:13–14

8. READ A BOOK…TO A DOG

I walked into the Levine Children's Hospital volunteer office, and the volunteer director asked me to visit an adult patient in the main building. After cruising skyward and stepping off the elevator, Sophie and I turned left and walked toward the nurses' station.

As Sophie approached one of the nurses, she began to show her delight with that familiar tail wag. Her tail is black, but the last four inches or so look as if her tail had been dipped in white paint. I love watching Sophie's tail wag—it is her way of communicating to the world that she is happy or pleased. Have you ever watched your dog wag its tail? I mean really, really stare at it and attempt to decipher what the dog is saying with its tail? I encourage you to try this with your dog. I can almost guarantee it will bring a smile to your face. It does to mine.

After quick introductions, Sophie entertained a large group of nurses with her trick routine. Lots of smiles and joy could be seen from the nurses. You see, dog-therapy visits are great for the staff too. After Sophie completed her trick routine and bows, we headed off to visit two adult patients.

We walked into a hospital room where there was an older woman. When she saw Sophie, her eyes lit up, followed by a beautiful smile. She was happy to see Sophie and appeared normal. But her mind and memory were slowly slipping because of a brain tumor. Sophie made her day, to say the least. On we went.

There he was in a loosely fitted hospital gown, sitting in a chair adjacent to his hospital bed. After introductions, he immediately began to pet Sophie. I looked down, and I saw multiple IVs on both arms. He began to tell me about his two dogs and his pet squirrel. We made some small talk, and then he began to swipe his phone right to left, right to left, and I could see the photos swishing by on his cell phone, thinking he was going to show me photos of his dogs and his pet squirrel. He stopped at an X-ray photo.

As he pointed at the photo, he told me hesitantly that this was his spine with cancer; he also had breast cancer. My emotions kicked in as my mind attempted to gather this information and make sense of it. My heart hurt for him. My gaze wandered and stopped at an object on the table. It was a book, *100 Things to Do in Charlotte Before You Die*. This visit was coming quickly into perspective. I attempted to maintain my demeanor, and my mind was attempting to process it all.

We talked some more, and before Sophie and I departed, I told him he would be in my prayers.

We received another request to visit a young girl, eight years old. As Sophie and I entered her room, her grandmother was lifting her legs on some stuffed animals to provide her comfort. She was a sweet little girl with a bubbly personality. Our conversation led to Sophie entertaining this young girl and her grandmother with tricks. Once we finished, the little girl asked me if she could read a book to my Sophie. I said, "Absolutely!"

As Sophie jumped up on the bed, leaning against the little girl's feet, her grandmother searched for a dog book that the girl wanted to read to Sophie. The young girl reached down with her hands and pulled the pant legs of her PJs toward her upper body to pull her legs up and give Sophie more room at the foot of the bed. It became obvious to me that the little girl used a wheelchair and had no leg function.

The grandmother couldn't find the dog book, and I told the girl that she could read a different book to Sophie. The little girl wouldn't have it…she wanted to read the dog book to Sophie. Grandmother found the right book, and the little girl began to read to Sophie. She read the book from the front cover all the way to the back cover. My heart was filled with joy as I watched this bubbly eight-year-old girl, unable to use her legs, read in such a delightful and joyful manner to Sophie. Pure innocence and love. It touched my heart deeply.

Sophie relaxing and listening to a dog story.

"The little girl asked me if she could read a book to my Sophie. I said, 'Absolutely!'"

Even a child is known by his deeds, Whether what he does is pure and right.

Prov. 20:11

9. SMILING EYES

I stopped at the nurses' station as I typically do and asked if they had a child in mind who would enjoy a therapy-dog visit. The first nurse turned to her colleague and said, "Do you think room number three would enjoy a visit from Sophie?" The second nurse replied, "He would love a visit from Sophie!" I replied with a thank you, and my eyes moved upward, seeing the room 6 sign above the door behind the nurses station. I turned to my left, and Sophie followed as we counted down the room numbers and arrived at room number 3. I knocked.

With Sophie sitting at my left side, I pushed the door open just enough to fit my head between the door and the jamb. I could see Sophie peeking inside just like I was. I asked, "Would you like a therapy-dog visit?" The mother said yes. I pushed the door open, and Sophie entered slightly ahead of me. I saw smiles from Mom and Dad, and to the left sat a young boy in his hospital gown in bed. I saw the steel rods, wires, and screws surrounding his head, locking his jaw and preventing his mouth from closing. Even with this postoperative condition, Bennett's bright eyes locked on to Sophie, and he spoke the best he could, with many gestures.

Introductions were made, and I asked the family if they would like to see Sophie do some tricks. Amy, Bennett's mother, asked Bennett if he would like to see Sophie do her tricks, and he replied yes and nodded. His mother helped him off the bed to a large La-Z-Boy–style chair and placed a hearing-aid band around his head. There Bennett sat eagerly, eyes wide open, waiting for this black-and-white canine to begin entertaining.

It is truly in moments like this during a therapy-dog visit when I fight back the tears. His *eyes* said it all. He was overjoyed to see Sophie! Every now and then during the trick routine, I would look up at Bennett and see *smiles* in his eyes.

Bennett is your typical young lad falling a little on tough times. He loves to play with his Australian Shepherds Belle and Cora, especially tossing the Frisbee. He is a straight-A student and finds himself in the gifted and talented classes. Like many young kids having favorite things to do, Bennett's passions are drawing and playing the drums.

I could sense something very special about this family. Even with Bennett's current health state, they were obviously very positive and caring. My heart was filled with warmth, knowing that Sophie changed this family's mental state even if it was for only twenty to twenty-five minutes, pulling their concerns away from the sterile confines of a hospital room and the postoperative recovery of their sweet boy.

We exchanged good-byes, and Sophie and I walked out, closing the door behind us and edging ourselves along the long hallway wall. I squatted down, leaned my lower back against the wall, and petted Sophie, and she looked at me as if she could sense what I was about to do next. I said a prayer for Bennett and his family.

Bennett comforted by Sophie.

Amy sent us a photo along with a note. "Thank you for sharing Sophie with our son yesterday! She is such a smart and sweet girl. Your visit made his day. We are so grateful to you both for helping our family and others in their healing process. Makes our hearts so happy."

"Every now and then during the trick routine, I would look up at Bennett and see smiles in his eyes."

Not only so, but we also glory in our sufferings, because we know that suffering produces perseverance; perseverance, character; and character, hope. And hope does not put us to shame, because God's love has been poured out into our hearts through the Holy Spirit, who has been given to us.

Rom. 5:3–5

10. OUR PRECIOUS CHILDREN

I glanced at the back side of my hospital volunteer badge to view my six-digit access code for the computer sign-in at Levine. Once signed in, Sophie and I began our usual walk over to the children's side of the hospital. We passed the security guard post, where the guards always smiled and said hello. We saw many patients and families coming and going, and I could see smiles on many faces as they watched Sophie walk past them.

As we headed for the elevators, we came across a little girl and her mom walking in the direction of the exit. She looked familiar. I stopped and asked her if she would like to pet Sophie. Her mom said, "She was just asking about Sophie a couple of minutes ago." I smiled, knowing my hunch was correct; we had seen this precious young girl on previous visits. I know Sophie would have smiled too, if she understood that the little girl was asking about her earlier. I could sense today would be a good therapy-dog visit. The girl was five years old.

Sophie watched me move forward and swipe my badge to access the staff elevator and then press the button to select our floor level. The doors opened, and we stepped in. Several staff members petted Sophie as our feet (and paws) sank into the elevator floor as we moved skyward. Then before we knew it, we became light on our feet as if floating for a split second, finally settling as the doors opened. As if on cue, Sophie led me out and turned left. She knew where to go.

I knocked on a door that was partially open, leaned in, and asked if they would like a therapy-dog visit. As I turned my head toward the young man, I saw him say, "Sure." I slowly moved into the room. The young man was sitting in a specialized wheelchair. His head was held in a neck brace, and I recognized that he was a quadriplegic. I asked him his name, and he replied. I introduced myself and Sophie. He used a sip-and-puff device to suck or blow through a straw to control his wheelchair as he positioned it to better view Sophie and her tricks. He was seventeen years old.

We ventured to the rehab floor, where I met a young boy in a wheelchair being pushed by one of the nurses. As I said hello to him and introduced Sophie, I glanced at the long scar stitched across his head from his right ear, over the top of his head, and all the way to his left ear. His black hair made the scar very visible. He spent a few minutes petting Sophie and seemed to feel better with her at his side. He was fourteen years old.

While we talked with this fourteen-year-old boy, out of a doorway to our left came a younger boy accompanied by his nurse. He had a *big* smile on his face. The nurse said he had seen Sophie from inside the therapy room and came out to see her. The little boy was adorable. I asked the boys if they would like to see Sophie perform some of her tricks, and they said yes with excitement in their voices. After Sophie completed her trick routine, the young boy struggled as he wobbled back to his room. He was five years old.

As Sophie and I waited in the hallway to enter another room, out of the corner of my eye, I saw a nurse pushing a baby crib, followed by two women. As the crib neared me, *it felt like everything went into slow motion.* The front of the crib began to pass me, and I looked inside and saw this beautiful infant lying on her back. The infant looked lifeless, like a white porcelain doll. Her white skin was flawless. The infant's right hand was resting on her right cheek. It was the most beautiful sight I had ever seen. As the crib and infant passed me, it was as if the infant glowed. As the two adults passed me, the slow-motion feeling dissipated. At that moment, I was trying to figure out in my mind what had just happened. It was a feeling I have never experienced before. It was amazing! The baby must have been just a couple of months old.

I glanced in a waiting room and saw a large group of people—about a dozen adults and one young boy. One of the men was passing out lunch items. I asked if they would like to be entertained by Sophie while they ate lunch. "Of course," they replied. After Sophie's routine, the little boy took a photo with Sophie. One of the adults told me that the little boy's brother was having major surgery today. The support system was there for the little boy's brother. The little boy was eight years old. His brother having surgery was six years old.

Sophie and I arrived at the infusion area. Chemotherapy or infusion stations feature comfortable patient chairs and entertainment systems to make it more enjoyable while patients are receiving treatment. As I approached, I saw a young boy in a wheelchair with an IV port in his left chest. The young boy had a service dog. The service dog was a beautiful golden retriever.

In the adjacent room, I glanced at a young girl inside a large crib. She too had an IV port on her chest. She saw Sophie, and a big smile appeared. She shouted, "Doggie!" I wanted so much to tell her that *dog* spelled backward is *God*.

As I waited for the nurse to place the infusion apparatus into the young boy, I glanced to the left and saw some drawings.

They were obviously drawn by the young patients while they relaxed at their infusion stations and received treatments.

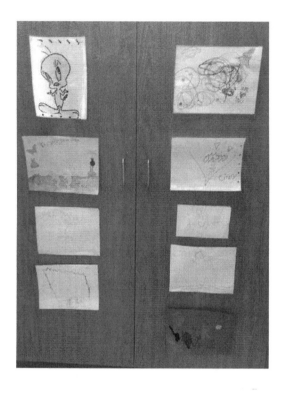

Wall of art from the heart.

Sophie performed her tricks, and then I brought Sophie over to the young boy for him to pet. The nurse picked up his right arm and hand and stroked Sophie's soft coat for a minute or two. The boy smiled widely and made some sounds of happiness. The young girl stood up in her crib as Sophie stood on her hind legs with front paws on the crib to allow the little girl to pet her. The little girl was a bit timid of

Sophie and did not pet her. The boy was ten years old. The little girl was three years old.

I leave the Levine children's hospital after every visit feeling so blessed that my children and I are healthy. God has blessed me with this wonderful canine companion. He put Sophie in my path for a reason. This is the reason. I know that Sophie brings temporary emotional relief to each of these youngsters and their families during her visits. These young boys and girls struggle every day. God bless them all.

"It was the most beautiful sight I had ever seen.

But those who hope in the Lord will renew their strength. They will soar on wings like eagles; they will run and not grow weary, they will walk and not be faint.

Isa. 40:31

11. THE AMAZING GRACE

A special therapy-dog request to visit room 1014 had come on a sticky note to Sophie and me. Sophie doesn't distinguish between color or gender, healthy or sick. Sophie loves unconditionally, and what is more important, I believe Sophie can feel the love from each and every person she comes in contact with. That day Sophie met a wonderful and bright young teen, Grace. Sophie performed her trick routine to the delight of Grace, her mother, Yvonne, and Grace's aunt. Grace said that she loved all animals, and her smile and snuggles with Sophie said it all.

Grace was a character with lots of personality. She would always voice her opinion and in a tactful manner. I remember Yvonne saying if you knew Grace personally, you knew she always had an opinion. She didn't want to be your hero. She would say to everyone, "I'm simply Grace. Battling cancer doesn't make me a hero. It makes me very unlucky. Everyone keeps telling me I'm going to beat this and keep staying positive. What if I don't beat it? Maybe that's my destiny. God's plan for me."

Grace had a puppy called Jesse. Grace asked me to help train her dog to become a therapy dog just like Sophie. This was Grace's wish. Several months elapsed, and I received a phone call from Grace's father, Sean. We scheduled a private basic obedience course to begin in several weeks at Grace's home to begin training Jesse.

Several days before the training was to start, I sent an e-mail to Sean as a schedule reminder for training. He replied that Grace was back in the hospital with a brain bleed. She was not doing well. My heart dropped.

I threw on Sophie's leash and collar, and we departed the next morning to see Grace. She appeared to be doing well and enjoyed Sophie's visit. We talked more about training Jesse to become a registered therapy dog.

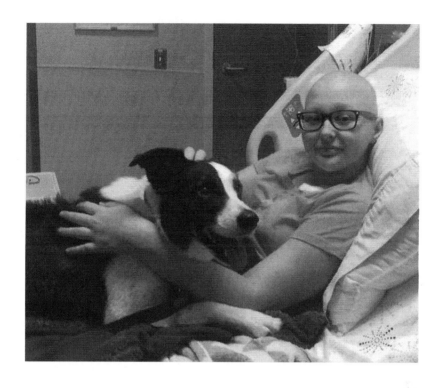

Grace's very first visit with Sophie.

Several days passed, and I learned from Sean that Grace had taken a turn for the worse. She was in a coma, and the prognosis was grim. I was deeply saddened.

I arrived the following day with Sophie. We stood outside Grace's hospital room for what seemed like hours, but it was only about fifteen minutes. Doctors, nurses, patients, and family members passed by and through. Then Sean emerged from Grace's room. We shook hands and hugged. He said I could go in but to leave Sophie outside. I entered Grace's room.

I saw Yvonne sitting on the bench seat adjacent to the window and immediately teared up. I could see the pain on her face and in her heart as she anticipated losing her daughter. We hugged. We spoke. I turned to Grace, tears running down my face. Hoping that she could hear me, I told her that we all loved her. I hugged Yvonne and walked out of the room. I hugged Sean and began my long walk down the hospital corridors. I cried, stopped crying, and cried some more.

My heart was broken. I wanted that one chance to take Grace and Jesse to a health organization and let them be a therapy-dog team. I wanted it so much but never got the chance to fulfill her wish.

I received a text from Sean saying that, after twenty-two months of battling osteosarcoma, Grace lost the fight against cancer at the young age of fourteen. In memory of Grace, I asked three absolutely wonderful friends to join me in packing Christmas shoe boxes at Samaritan's Purse in Charlotte.

The day Grace passed, I prayed at my bedside. I asked Grace to let me know she was OK and to give me a sign that she was in heaven. The following day after my friends and I finished volunteering at Samaritan's Purse Christmas shoe box program, a dear friend (Whitney) gave me a Christmas gift basket from her and her family. It was filled with a Christmas ornament, food items, dog toys, a coffee mug, and other items.

After sorting through the gift basket, I lifted the coffee mug. The mug was beautiful. It had a picture of a bicycle on one side and "Merry Christmas" on the other. Then I flipped the coffee mug over to view the bottom, and with astonishment, I saw that "Grace" was written there. Was Grace sending me the sign I had prayed for? Then a Facebook friend recognized another sign. The Christmas ornament Whitney gave to me was a red, white, and green round ornament with the large letter K (K for my last name). The friend suggested that the round ornament represented the letter O and, combined with the letter K, it meant OK. Putting all of this together revealed, "*Grace OK!*" My heart was singing with joy as I knew Grace had heard my prayer, and she indeed sent me her message.

I believe God sends messengers to us all. We just have to be able to recognize them. On this very special day, my friend Whitney was the messenger. There is absolutely no doubt in my mind that Grace is OK and in heaven. And sometimes those who leave us will leave us messages as well. Grace did, with her handwritten notes left inside her Bible. "I know you don't have an answer now but keep trusting in God."

Sophie and I visited Grace's grave site after attending her celebration of life event. There we stood all alone with Grace at her final resting place overflowing with flowers. I cried and talked to her. Sophie left her children's hospital ID card on the temporary grave marker as a gift for Grace.

Grace sent the message that she is OK.

The Christmas ornament message, OK.

Months passed, and I received a phone call from Yvonne. She was ready to work with Jesse so they could become a therapy-dog team. I was delighted. After completing their handler's test and three observations, Yvonne and Jesse are now a registered therapy-dog team.

Grace's wish was for Jesse to become a therapy dog (Yvonne and Jesse).

I know Grace will be looking down on her mom and puppy with lots of smiles. Rest in peace, young lady, and play with all the therapy dogs in heaven to your heart's content. Amazing Grace, I know you are OK with our Lord.

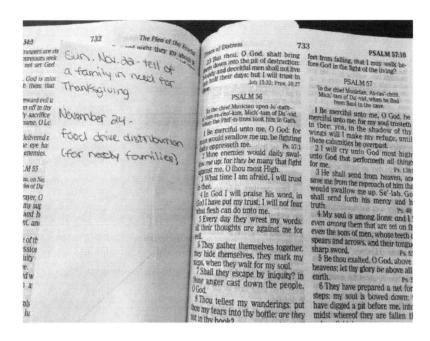

Grace often placed personal notes (messages) in her Bible.

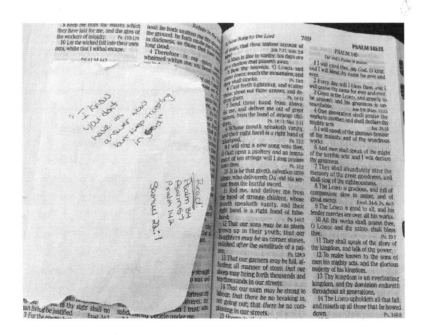

More notes left by amazing Grace.

"There is absolutely no doubt in my mind that Grace is OK and in heaven."

Jesus said to her, "I am the resurrection and the life. The one who believes in me will live, even though they die."

John 11:25

12. A TEAR

As we approached room 1201, I saw a lovely woman sit up ever so quickly—like a child in a candy store, with her eyes wide and bright—along with a beautiful smile when she saw Sophie. I asked if they would like a therapy-dog visit, and Pat and her daughter, Nikki, smiled with excitement and said, "Yes!"

As Sophie sat along Pat's bedside, Nikki said to her mother, "Sophie came to see you, Mom." Pat began to tear up with joy. She raised her right hand to stop a tear that had made it halfway down her right cheek. That tiny tear was filled with an enormous amount of happiness. My heart felt the compassion and love Pat had not only for Sophie but also for animals in general. It was another one of those special and rare moments that will be captured in my heart forever. Pat asked if Sophie could get up in the bed with her. I said, "Of course."

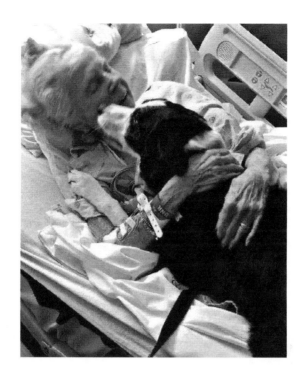

A big hug from Pat and a big kiss from Sophie.

Weeks later I received a request from hospice to visit Pat on her eighty-ninth birthday. We were delighted! Pat looked fantastic, and of course, requests came in for Sophie to perform her trick routine. For her birthday, Sophie presented Pat with a photo of them together.

Pat holding a birthday gift from Sophie.

Several months after Pat's eighty-ninth birthday party, Nikki sent me a note that Pat's health had deteriorated and that she had passed away. Pat's ashes were spread on their family-owned property of six acres atop a mountain. Sophie sent a small garden rock to be placed on the mountaintop with Pat. On the engraved garden rock, it says, "Pat, I miss you, and I will see you again someday! Love, Sophie."

"Pat began to tear up with joy. She raised her right hand to stop a tear that had made it halfway down her right cheek."

Even to your old age and gray hairs I am he, I am he who will sustain you. I have made you and I will carry you; I will sustain you and I will rescue you.

Isa. 46:4

13. HEARTSTRINGS

Sophie and I were embarking on our regularly scheduled therapy-dog visits today. As we ventured farther into the hospital, we arrived at the elevators, where we gained some altitude to our first visiting floor. Turning several corners and swiping the keypad for the automatic doors to open, we approached one of the rooms in the infusion section. We saw a little girl smiling, and she shouted, "Sophie!" This immediately brought smiles to our faces. This little girl was so happy and eager to see Sophie again, she began to creep out of her chair along with her IV still hooked up. She began to give Sophie commands to do tricks, followed by "Good girl!" After Sophie completed her amazing trick routine, the little girl wanted to walk Sophie on her leash. So Sophie, the little girl, and I walked the halls of the hospital. So precious! So cute! Such a personality in this young girl, who was cheerful despite her health issues.

We moved on to several other floors and rooms, meeting remarkable families and patients. One little boy was going to have brain surgery the next day. Another little boy was not quite in the mood to have a therapy-dog visit today. A teenage boy wearing a helmet also walked with Sophie and me up and down the halls. Another teen, who struggled to walk, watched patiently as Sophie performed her tricks. Since the teen was unable to bend down, I stood next to this teen and prompted Sophie to stand on her hind legs with her front legs on my waist so the teen could reach and pet Sophie. A smile emerged.

Our final visit was a personal request on the adult side of Levine, where we were taken upward in the elevator once again. Sophie treated the nursing staff on this floor with her usual entertainment, which they enjoyed while several loved all over Sophie. We moved across the hall for another visit.

As we approached the doorway, I saw a woman lying calmly in her hospital bed. The young woman was unable to pet Sophie on her own, so I called Sophie over to stand on her hind legs and place her paws on the hospital bed. The woman was unable to move her head due to neck braces nor her arms, so I took the woman's hand, placed it on Sophie's head, and moved her hand back and forth on Sophie's head. As I glanced to my right toward the young woman's face, I saw a big smile. Although her pretty eyes stared directly toward the ceiling, they were wide open as if to communicate that she loved Sophie. Another moment. A moment I will never forget.

Our visit came to an end, but there would be many more. We left with memories and moments that captured our attention and pulled on our heartstrings. We should feel so lucky to have our good health and should never take it for granted.

"I took the woman's hand, placed it on Sophie's head, and moved her hand back and forth on Sophie's head."

Then your light shall break forth like the morning, Your healing shall spring forth speedily, And your righteousness shall go before you; The glory of the Lord shall be your rear guard.

Isaiah 58:8

14. CHILDREN ARE LIKE PUPPIES

I was on my computer searching for a place to volunteer my time on Thanksgiving Day one year, and I found this local nonprofit organization. I made a couple of calls, and on Thanksgiving Day, I had the opportunity to work with Chef Eva and help prepare Thanksgiving meals for the staff and residents.

Chef Eva and I prepped Thanksgiving dinner for the residents.

Adjacent to Levine Children's Hospital, where Sophie and I frequent, sits Florence Crittenton Services. Florence

Crittenton Services provides health, education, and social services to at-risk or pregnant adolescents and women and their families.

After volunteering on Thanksgiving Day, I spoke with the volunteer coordinator, and Sophie began making occasional therapy-dog visits for the staff and residents. On several occasions during our visits, some of the young moms had their children with them.

Children are like puppies in many ways. Raising a child is similar to raising a puppy. Both have to be potty-trained. Both need to be trained in discipline and respect. Both will at times refuse to do what they are told. And it is important that the training for both puppy and child is consistent to ensure they learn and exhibit good behavior.

It is interesting to watch these young children watch an energetic canine like Sophie run around and perform tricks. Their eyes show bewilderment like a puppy seeing a cat for the first time. The children's bodies freeze in amazement like a puppy hearing its first squeaky toy. Some children look up at their moms as if to say, "What is going on here," just like a puppy tilts his head when he hears someone whistle for the first time. Some of the children get scared and run to the comfort and safety of their moms just like a puppy scurries away when hearing fireworks or thunder. All in all, the children appear to enjoy this spectacle of a dog doing weird things like a human.

What kind of weird things? Sitting pretty, playing dead, rolling over, walking alongside me on her two hind legs, picking up her toys and placing them one by one in a backpack, responding to the command "under arrest" by standing on her two hind legs and placing her front paws on the wall while I pat her down like a police officer making an arrest, crisscrossing and weaving through the legs, understanding counting to the number three, and so on. So imagine a youngster who has never seen a dog before, and this dog can do all of this. Wow! Well, most adults haven't seen this either.

"The children's bodies freeze in amazement like a puppy hearing its first squeaky toy."

Train up a child in the way he should go, And when he is old he will not depart from it.

Prov. 22:6

15. PAULA'S BEST FRIEND

Paula trains as a marathon runner. At the time I met her, she was training for an out-of-state relay race with some friends. I have never run a marathon and can only imagine the amount of training that must be undertaken to excel at such an extreme level of fitness.

When not in training or participating in a running event, Paula enjoys hanging out with her friends. One of her best friends is Murray. One day Murray and his pal Jade took off running behind a new boarder (horse) on the 155-acre farm. Not a good idea.

Murray's cry was heard throughout the farm. The horse reared up and kicked Murray on the left side of his face. His head was swollen, both eyes were shut, and there was blood coming from his eyes, nose, and mouth. Paula's sister-in-law came to Murray's rescue and transported him to the doctor.

X-rays showed fifty plus fractures to Murray's skull and nose cavity. Miraculously, there were no brain or jaw injuries that could have been fatal. The fractures were allowed to heal on their own like a jigsaw puzzle. Murray would lose his left eye in the accident. This was difficult indeed for Paula and her family—and their best friend.

You see, Paula's best friend Murray is a golden retriever who was five years old when this incident occurred. I should rephrase that and say that Murray is a *tough* golden retriever. Many years after his injury, I received a call from this tough golden's owner and handler, Paula. She was interested in becoming a therapy-dog team.

Weighing in at nearly one hundred pounds and twelve years old now, Murray went through the standard protocol of therapy dog testing and observing and passed with flying colors. Murray has the sweet demeanor that makes an exceptional therapy dog. He is a gentle giant. Murray doesn't know that he is disabled. He is simply being a dog like any other dog.

Murray at five years old.
(photo courtesy of Whitney Gray Photography).

Photo by Hope Rogers

Dog days of summer at the library
Jalynn York reads a book to her canine friend, Murray, at the Lois Morgan Edwards Memorial Library on July 21 as Murray's owner, Paula Fox, looks on. During the summer, children are encouraged to Paws-Awhile-To-Read on Thursday afternoons. For details, call 704-624-2828.

Murray at his first public affairs event (courtesy of Home News, *Marshville, NC).*

In only a matter of months, Murray was able to start his own therapy-dog gig. Yes, he found his calling. He now attends his local library (Edwards Memorial Library in Marshville, North Carolina), where children are encouraged to read to him every week. This program makes reading fun and at the same time enhances the reading skills of our youngsters. The title of the program is "Paws Awhile to Read." How creative! Well done, Paula and Murray. Keep *running* therapy-dog team full steam ahead! And I don't mean running after horses!

A star is born.

"Murray doesn't know that he is disabled. He is simply being a dog like any other dog."

A friend loves at all times, and a brother is born for a time of adversity.

Prov. 17:17

16. UNCONDITIONAL LOVE

Sophie and I pulled up to an old brick building housing the Life Choices group of Holy Angels. Holy Angels provides specialized round-the-clock care for children and adults with intellectual development disabilities and delicate medical conditions. The unconditional love each of them shows toward Sophie is wonderful and heartwarming.

Sophie jumped out of the old Nissan truck and immediately moved toward the building. She lowered her head in that common border collie crouch and placed her wet black nose near the crack of the door, her tail wagging, as she knew who was inside.

We entered, and a dozen or more Life Choices group participants and staff cheered, "It's Sophie!" This group was interactive with Sophie; they got to perform trick routines with her—letting her weave between their legs, telling her she was under arrest and patting her down like they were police officers, sitting pretty, and walking Sophie on the leash. We ventured outside, and they tossed a Frisbee. One of their favorite routines was holding hula hoops and having Sophie jump through them.

Life Choices group holding hoops for Sophie.

The group absolutely adores Sophie, and on one visit, they gave Sophie a Christmas present, a paper loop chain countdown to Christmas day. Sophie's favorite gift was a water bowl to which they added some personal touches. How sweet is that? Their love for Sophie is unconditional. Sophie barks back, saying, "Ditto!"

If Sophie could talk to the Life Choice's group, here is what she would say: "Thank you so much for letting me visit each and every one of you. You are all kind and thoughtful to me and Rob. I enjoy so much when you do tricks with me, especially when you hold the hula hoops so I can jump through them. I personally thank each of you—Samantha, Sarah, Leslie, Kyle, Edwin, Robert, Elise, Katie, Maria,

Martha, Taylor, Christina, Dawn, Kelly, and Tommy—for making me feel welcome each time I visit. Love, Sophie."

Custom designed water bowl made especially for Sophie.

"We entered, and a dozen or more Life Choices group participants and staff cheered, "It's Sophie!"

Love is patient, love is kind. It does not envy, it does not boast, it is not proud. It does not dishonor others, it is not self-seeking, it is not easily angered, it keeps no record of wrongs. Love does not delight in evil but rejoices with the truth. It always protects, always trusts, always hopes, always perseveres.

1 Cor. 13:4–7

17. A TOUCH

I have a passion for road cycling. For those not familiar with the term, it means bicycling on the road. We are called roadies. Roadies can be found riding ordinary aluminum-frame bikes to expensive carbon-graphite-frame bikes on the thinnest wheels you can imagine.

I do some minor repairs on my own bike when I can, but in most instances, I take it to the local bike shop as there is some maintenance I simply cannot do on my own. I own a carbon fiber Trek Madone 6.5 SSL, a lightweight bicycle weighing a whopping 15.5 pounds, with the frame weighing in at 1.96 pounds. It's a much needed lightweight frame for when I climbed those mountains in the Asheville area back in the day.

Someone else who loves bicycles is Oscar, whom Sophie and I visit at the Courtland Terrace retirement nursing center. When we arrived this day, there was Kim Griffin Burke waiting for us. As always, Kim had a big beautiful smile and loved all over Sophie as if she were her own canine companion.

Kim led us to our good friend Oscar, who was sitting back relaxing in his La-Z-Boy–style lounge chair with his sunglasses on while he spoke into the handheld microphone on the ham radio. Ham radio means "amateur radio." In his earlier ham operator days, Oscar would talk with other ham operators from around the world. A hobby that he loves and enjoys.

I entered the room with Sophie and announced that Sophie and I were there. Oscar always replied, "Oh, Sophie," accompanied by a smile. I walked Sophie over to Oscar's chair, and Sophie stood on her hind legs and placed her front legs on Oscar's lap, so Oscar could give Sophie some good hugs and petting.

Believe it or not, Oscar is a young ninety-eight years old. He grew up near Montgomery, Alabama. He was one of ten siblings. He was raised with four brothers and five sisters, five of whom have lived into their nineties. Amazing longevity DNA, I told Oscar.

Growing up, Oscar worked in a textile plant where the company wove cloth. He operated a stitcher machine that attached two cloths into one piece. At one point while working at the textile plant, he asked to work the second or

Rob Kortus

third shift in order to complete high school, which he did,
barely.

Sophie loves Oscar.

As a young man, Oscar came down with an eye infection.
Doctors evidently had a hard time clearing the infection. By
the age of twenty-two, Oscar had lost all his vision. He
finished high school just before becoming disabled with
blindness.

Before Oscar's blindness, a man named Morris Frank, blind
himself, founded the Seeing Eye organization, which began

97

in 1928 and was incorporated the following year (www.seeingeye.org). The organization, which breeds seeing-eye dogs, finally settled down in 1965 in Morris Township, New Jersey. The sixty-acre campus is home to all the admin offices, a veterinary clinic, dog kennels, and student residences. Seeing Eye is the oldest guide-dog school still in existence in the world.

Oscar visited Seeing Eye in 1943 and left with his seeing-eye dog, Neal. He had Neal for more than ten years, and after the loss of Neal, he went back a second time and found another service dog, Eva, whom he had for four years. Neal would guide Oscar for half a mile from his home to the textile mill, where Oscar was able to continue working in another department after his blindness.

Oscar with his first service dog, Neal.

With the help of his brother-in-law, in a side building adjacent to his garage, Oscar set up a small shop repairing bicycles. His disability was not stopping Oscar from living a normal life. In fact, Oscar could build and true a wheel with no assistance. Oscar had the little bicycle repair shop in Cramerton, North Carolina, from 1947 to 1962.

On one visit to see Oscar, I took some bicycle tools and my road bike to Oscar's small room in the nursing home for him to check them out…it was beautiful to see him handle and touch the bike and tools and a honor to hear him reminisce about days past handling and repairing bicycles. He was simply delighted by the visit and intrigued with today's bicycle technology. My good friend Oscar, may you live in splendid health for many more years.

"Oscar always replied, "Oh, Sophie," accompanied by a smile."

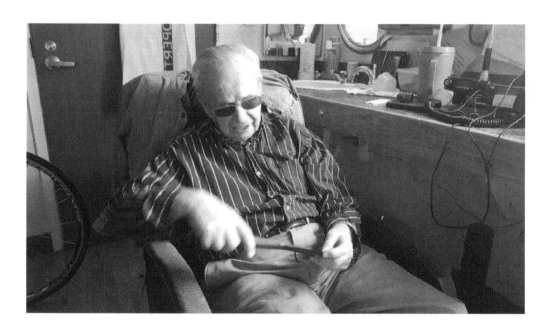

Oscar checking out today's high tech bicycle tools.

Oscar is amazed by the lightweight carbon fiber bikes of today.

Blessed is the one who perseveres under trial because, having stood the test, that person will receive the crown of life that the Lord has promised to those who love him.

James 1:12

18. LOSS AND GAIN

I turned the steering wheel left to turn my truck into Camp Cherokee, the venue for Camp Luck Kids. Camp Luck's mission is to improve the lives of kids and their families who are coping with congenital heart disease and empowering each kid to live life to their fullest. As I looked left and right through the open windows of the truck, I felt the beauty and calmness of the slowly moving branches and leaves on the hundreds of trees blown by the free-flowing wind inside Kings Mountain State Park. My right hand moved over the gearshift, and I slid the shifter forward into park mode. I exited the vehicle, flipped my backpack over my right shoulder, and lifted the hatchback to release Sophie into this wilderness of beauty.

Off in the distance was Kim Jackson awaiting my arrival. After a greeting, we were off to the mess hall to wait for the kids to arrive from their daily events so they could meet Sophie. While in the mess hall, Sophie entertained the volunteer administrative staff, and they thoroughly enjoyed her tricks. The kids began to trickle in. We gathered briefly for a group photo with Sophie, and the kids quickly disappeared back into the beautiful landscape.

Sophie and I were off to visit the kids after they dispersed to their activity stations. We visited the kids at the lake who were donning their life vests to go canoeing but without first watching Sophie run through her trick routine and catch the Frisbee thrown by the kids. Tired and hot, Sophie lay in several inches of the lake water to cool off.

After the lake visit, Sophie and I meandered along the trail to find the upcoming junior leadership team discussing how to tackle an obstacle while standing shoulder to shoulder on a log. I watched with enjoyment as about a dozen teens were standing on this log and discussing how to move one of them from one end of the log to the other without placing his or her feet on the ground. During a break, Sophie performed for the next generation counselors, and they loved her.

I had the opportunity to learn more about Camp Luck from Kim. Kim is the program coordinator and one of the cofounders of Camp Luck Kids. My first question was, why did she assist in creating such a wonderful organization? Her son Jacob was one of the many kids who had congenital heart disease, and he too helped create the camp.

Born with heart disease, Jacob was a wiry kid, and full of energy at seventeen years old. He was very funny and loved to make people laugh, always smiling around everyone even with a stent in his heart to aid in keeping a heart valve open. He loved his dog Ozzy, an Australian shepherd who was full of energy and in a sense a therapy dog for Jacob. In fact, he loved to write "Ozzy Rox" on everything.

Jacob enjoyed throwing out actor Chuck Norris facts so he could make and watch people laugh. Kim told me that a quote from actor Brad Garrett summed up Jacob's life. "You take away all the other luxuries in life, and if you can make someone smile and laugh, you have given the most special gift, happiness." Kim went on to say that this was exactly how Jacob lived his life. Jacob even found it easy to laugh at himself.

I had the honor of meeting Dr. René Herlong at Camp Luck while watching the kids play Ga-ga in the octagonal ring, a form of dodgeball but only using the hands and rolling one ball. He is a Camp Luck cofounder and chief of pediatric cardiology at the Sanger Heart and Vascular Institute. He has worked at Camp Cherokee for thirty-five-plus years. I felt his passion and commitment while he spoke about camp life. He envisions Camp Luck as being Jacob's legacy. This is what Dr. Herlong desires the camp to reflect.

The driving force behind Kim to assist in establishing Camp Luck Kids and volunteering was very personal. Camp Luck

Kids will always be a reminder of her wonderful and loving son who never left the house or anywhere without giving her a kiss and hug even in front of his friends. When Jacob was asked whether he would change the fact that he had heart disease, Jacob quickly replied with confidence, "No, everything happens for a reason."

Camp Luck kids and staff with Sophie.

Although the loss of Jacob after complications during his ninth heart surgery at the age of seventeen brought sadness to many, there are many gains that have been made and will continue from his legacy. His mom, Kim, Dr. Herlong, and many others will ensure Jacob's legacy thrives well into the future.

Jacob Jackson (1993–2010) and his canine companion, Ozzy.

"He loved his dog Ozzy, an Australian shepherd full of energy and in a sense a therapy dog for Jacob. In fact, he loved to write "Ozzy Rox" on everything."

My heart and flesh may fail, but God is the strength of my heart and my portion forever.

Psalm 73:26

19. I WANT TO BECOME A REGISTERED THERAPY-DOG TEAM

Statistics say there are forty-two million households in the United States that have one or more dogs. There are seventy-three million dogs in the world; a slice of the seventy-three million are strays. Imagine if all were therapy dogs. The world would be a much different place.

So you want to become a therapy-dog team? First, ask yourself if you have the motivation to give back in a volunteer capacity. Second, ask yourself if you have the time to volunteer. Third, ask yourself if your canine companion is a friendly and obedient dog. Finally, ask yourself if you have the desire to make it happen. If you answered yes to all of the above, then contact a therapy-dog organization and get on board.

Does your canine companion have the personality and capability to become a therapy dog? Is your dog 10 months old or older (minimum age requirement)? Does your dog

- listen actively,
- obey your commands,

- not jump on people,
- act friendly with people and other dogs,
- accept petting from children and adult strangers,
- not lick excessively, and
- walk on a leash without pulling?

If yes to all, your dog is a good candidate for therapy-dog work. If not, contact your local certified professional dog trainer and sign up for a basic obedience class.

You can begin your journey by visiting Invisible Paw Prints, Inc. The author founded this non-profit therapy dog testing and registry company after writing this book (www.invisiblepawprints.com). Becoming a therapy-dog team is simple. It only takes some time on your part. The service to test is absolutely free. When you do become a registered therapy-dog team, you will be covered with liability insurance carried by Invisible Paw Prints, Inc. The only cost is the annual membership fee.

So, are you ready for a new journey? Do you have the desire to make a difference in your life and your canine companion's life? Are you motivated enough to embark on a new and fascinating course? Your canine companion wants to work for you. Your dog cannot ask you to help him or her.

You have to take the necessary steps to do so. Remember, an obedient dog with a job is a joyful, caring, and happy dog. These are the types of dogs that can make your life not only productive but also much easier.

"Finally, ask yourself if you have the desire to make it happen."

Each of you should give what you have decided in your heart to give, not reluctantly or under compulsion, for God loves a cheerful giver.

2 Cor. 9:7

20. INVISIBLE PAW PRINTS

A fox and an arctic hare leave a winding trail of paw prints through the snow, carved between beautiful spruce trees on the frozen tundra. A mother bear and her cubs leave their familiar paw prints along the wooded trail in the dense forest.

Therapy dogs will not leave any physical trail, no paw prints—only *invisible paw prints* in every facility that they visit. Therapy dogs leave trails of *smiles, happiness, hope, and love.*

Sophie, you are a gift from above and a true *blessing* to me. Thank you, Lord, for this wonderful animal whom you have placed in my path. I am ever so grateful for this gift. I know your plan was for Sophie and me to be together, because we were the perfect team to fulfill your plan to give back by volunteering to make a difference in people's lives, especially those who are battling illness.

Sophie has become a unique therapy dog. She entertains, and this is why she has become so well liked and ingrained in the memories of those who come in contact with her. She reveals her intelligence and affection to everyone she meets. One can sum Sophie's life up as a rags-to-riches story. Found lost in the woods, undernourished, underweight, ill, thirsty, alone, and scared. Brought back to good health, trained in obedience, she is now filled with the richness of giving back in one way a canine can, through the blessing of being a loving and affectionate therapy dog.

This book is not only about the journey of a therapy-dog team but also, and more important, about how God provides guidance in our lives. How God plans our lives and sends us messages (nudges) that we need to learn how to recognize, especially the messengers who provide us with the clues. How God answers our prayers. How volunteering is important in our daily lives as God directs us and how God touches our personal lives. All for God's glory.

A blessing from our dear Lord, beautiful Sophie.

This is a book for the young and old alike, designed to be inspirational for readers so that maybe today or tomorrow they will seek volunteering opportunities in whatever capacity they desire in order to give something back for everything that God has given them.

"How volunteering is important in our daily lives as God directs us and how God touches our personal lives. All for God's glory."

And as for you, brothers and sisters, never tire of doing what is good.

Acts 20:35

ABOUT THE AUTHOR

Robin (Rob) Kortus spent twenty-seven-plus years in military aviation. Of those years, he spent over ten years as an enlisted man in the army repairing helicopters; he also served as a warrant officer and as a pilot flying Blackhawks. Immediately after leaving the army, Rob received his commission in the US Coast Guard (CG), where he became an instructor pilot / flight examiner. After seventeen-plus years in the CG, Rob retired as a CG commander.

From left to right, Wallace, Sophie, and Sulley.

After his retirement from flying, he became an entrepreneur and founded three small businesses, JerseyBin.com, Commander in Leash Dog Obedience & Behavior Training, and after writing his book, Rob founded Invisible Paw Prints,

Inc. Rob currently resides in Charlotte, North Carolina, with his three loyal canine companions, Sophie, Sulley, and Wallace.

Sophie the border collie was rescued in Asheville, North Carolina, when she was about ten months old by Brother Wolf Animal Rescue. As of the printing of this book, she is seven years old. The journey continues for Sophie, who will continue to leave no paw prints, only trails of human smiles, happiness, hope, and love. She will leave *invisible paw prints* in every facility she visits. Some will never know she was there. *Those who meet Sophie will never forget her.*

Therapy-dog team Rob and Sophie.

Please visit www.invisiblepawprints.com to become a fellow therapy-dog team. Join Rob Kortus and Sophie the border collie in a tremendous journey where you will realize the power of giving back in a manner you would never realize would be so gratifying, so rewarding, so precious.

Rob Kortus

Life always has a way to move forward.

How will you move forward in your life?

What will be your legacy?

Out of his fullness we have all received grace in place of grace already given.

John 1:16

To my beloved Sophie. I love you.

Made in the USA
Middletown, DE
04 June 2017